KENT'S TRANSPORT HERITAGE

JAMES PRESTON

AMBERLEY

First published 2017

Amberley Publishing
The Hill, Stroud,
Gloucestershire, GL5 4EP

www.amberley-books.com

Map illustration by Thomas Bohm, User Design, Illustration and Typesetting.

ISBN: 978 1 4456 6991 5 (print)
ISBN: 978 1 4456 6992 2 (ebook)

British Library Cataloguing in Publication Data.
A catalogue record for this book is available from the British Library.

Typeset in 10pt on 13pt Celeste.
Origination by Amberley Publishing.
Printed in the UK.

Contents

Introduction

Transport facilities in Kent have been of national as well as local significance given the county's proximity to both the capital, London, and to the European mainland. These have evolved particularly over the past 250 years to meet economic and social change and to embrace technological innovation in steam power, the internal combustion engine, and the use of electric power. Expanding trade influenced by the London market, increased personal mobility, and changing social factors such as the rise of the seaside day trip or holiday, commuting to work and foreign travel, have all left their mark.

Road transport saw the introduction of the turnpike in the eighteenth century after increased carriage and wagon traffic, and its demise in the nineteenth century in face of railway developments, while the twentieth-century rise in motor traffic led to improved roads and increased facilities. Street tramways providing cheap urban transport flourished briefly in the early twentieth century, only to disappear by the end of the 1930s.

A widespread network of railways developed after 1830 connecting, primarily, London with the Channel ports and the coast, but also via branch lines most areas of the county. Evolution of the railway system in the twentieth century has seen the high-speed railway not only link London with the continent, but also serve the Kent commuter traffic.

Cheap water-borne transport had been essential to carry the produce of Kent's agriculture and industries, particularly to the London market. The number of Thames sailing barges capable of berthing in small creeks peaked around 1900, remaining in use until the mid-twentieth century. Cross Channel passenger services provided by the rival railway companies promoted the development of Folkestone and Dover as ferry ports, as well as of Port Victoria and Queenborough Pier. Travel by rail and ferry in turn was replaced by the rise of the roll-on car ferry, briefly by hovercraft, and latterly by the Channel Tunnel shuttle train. Air transport, including car ferries from Lympne and Lydd, briefly flourished, but air travel from Kent has always been overshadowed by the London airports.

As with all evolving industries the older, obsolete facilities are in danger of disappearing or are already lost. There is virtually no trace of the tramways, railway branch lines have been lifted and disappeared, a few sailing barges are in preservation, and the wharves are often in decay. Sites become 'brown field', ripe for development, with airfields like Manston now under threat.

Roads

Roads through Kent had from Roman times a political and military importance, especially Watling Street, being the shortest route to mainland Europe. However, the roads decayed, and, in winter, were virtually impassable, especially on the heavy clays of the Weald. The poor state was partly due to the responsibility for maintenance devolving onto the parish, which was an inappropriate body for such a function. The increased use of wheeled vehicles in the seventeenth and early eighteenth centuries led to the emergence of the Turnpike Trust, who were responsible for the upkeep and improvement of roads and bridges in return for a toll. Kent's first turnpike, established in 1709, was for a section of the road to Rye that ran from Sevenoaks to Pembury with a branch via Tonbridge to the fashionable spa of Tunbridge Wells. In 1749 the road from London was improved with the turnpiking of the Farnborough to Sevenoaks section. After Tunbridge Wells the road to Hastings gave way to rutted and uneven tracks, and it was not until 1741 that the Pembury to Flimwell section was turnpiked; 1753 for the rest of the route, and 1762 for the road to Rye.

A total of sixty-two turnpike trusts were established in Kent, mostly in the second half of the eighteenth century. Some very late enactments included the Gravesend and Wrotham of 1825, with the last being the Cranbrook to Hawkhurst Trust in 1841. Turnpike trusts maintained varying lengths of road, the Kent average being just over 10 miles. Important routes such as the Dover road were not improved as a unit. The first section between Northfleet and Strood was enacted in 1711, becoming the Dartford and Strood Trust of 1738 maintaining 15 miles; the Chatham and Canterbury Trust of 1753 maintained 25 miles, while the Canterbury and Barham and the Dover and Barham Downs trusts, also of 1753, maintained 6 and 8 miles respectively. The gap of 2.5 miles between Strood and Chatham Hill was not filled until 1768 when an Act, passed against the wishes of Rochester Corporation, created a Commission of the Pavement to maintain the road in Rochester and with powers to build a 'New Road' to Chatham Hill, bypassing the squalid Chatham High Street. This Commission lasted until November 1876 when its debts were paid by the Rochester Bridge Trust and its toll gates removed. The movement of traffic away from roads with the spread of the railways undermined the financial viability of turnpike trusts, leading to their winding up and functions being adopted by local and central government.

The last turnpike trust to operate was the Biddenden to Boundgate (near Faversham) Trust which lasted from 1766 until 1884.

The turnpike trusts left a legacy of structures, including toll keepers' cottages, mile posts, and some bridges.

Toll Houses

The late eighteenth-century, octagonal toll house located near Bridge [TR 2233 4920] on the Canterbury to Barham section of the Dover road.

The toll house on Mereworth Road, Mereworth [TQ 6533 5337] is a late eighteenth-century, two-storey, octagonal building constructed in stone under a tiled roof for the Tonbridge and Maidstone Trust, which operated from 1765.

The late eighteenth-century toll house on the junction of Oxenhoath Road and Park Road, West Peckham [TQ 6268 5235], for the Tonbridge and Maidstone Trust route. This is a five-sided building facing north-east with a square back. It has Gothic windows, crenulation, and a single door to the front.

Toll Bar Cottage, Eynsford [TQ 5372 6566], is a sixteenth-century house that was used as a toll house on the turnpike road to Shoreham before the road was rerouted in 1861.

The single-storey toll house built in Gothic style between 1830 and 1840 at Bapchild [TQ 9281 6313] on the section of Watling Street controlled by Chatham and Canterbury Trust.

The early nineteenth-century, single-storey toll house built on an island in the road at Whitstable [TR 1050 6560]. This design has a projecting bay, giving a view from large windows along the road. This was situated at the Whitstable gate of the Whitstable and Canterbury Trust set up in 1736.

The early nineteenth-century, two-storey toll house on the junction of the Tenterden and Smarden roads at Headcorn [TQ 8420 4409], built for the Maidstone and Biddenden Trust of 1803.

The toll house at Biddenden [TQ 9543 3946]; although similar to that at Headcorn, with two bay windows, it differs in having the main door at the front.

The nineteenth-century toll house on the East Malling to Wateringbury road [TQ 6957 5476], operated by the East Malling and Pembury Green Turnpike.

Mile Posts

Mile post at West Malling [TQ 6835 5820] on the section of the London to Maidstone road operated by the Wrotham and Maidstone Trust of 1773.

Above: Milestone [TQ 7444 6381] erected on the Rochester and Maidstone turnpike of 1727.

Left: An eighteenth-century milestone in the High Street, Tenterden [TQ 8834 3329], stood beside the toll gate and toll house. The other face is inscribed 'Cranbrook 8 Rolvenden 3'.

A cast-iron mile post on the West Malling to Tonbridge road [TQ 6722 5641] with manufacturer's name.

Above: Mile post on Watling Street at Gillingham [TQ 7995 6643], which is maintained by the Chatham and Canterbury Trust.

Left: Mile post on the Maidstone to Marden road [TQ 7535 4579], operated by the Goudhurst and Stylebridge Trust of 1765.

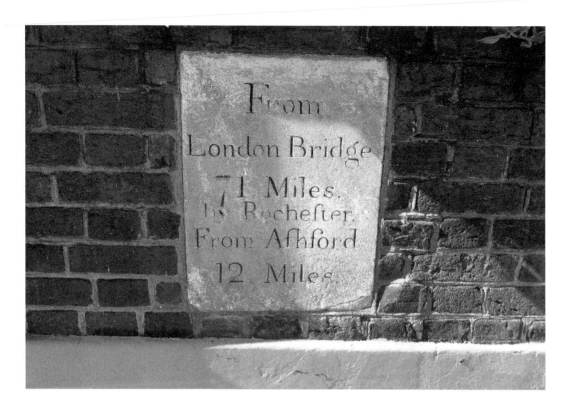

Above: Milestone on the wall of the Swan Hotel, Hythe [TR 1605 3479].

Right: Milestone at Charing [TQ 9454 4990] by the Ashford and Maidstone turnpike of 1793.

Bridges

The medieval bridge at Aylesford [TQ 7294 5892], thought to have been constructed around 1250, which features pedestrian refuges on either side. The two centre arches were replaced by a single arch in 1824 to facilitate barge traffic to Maidstone – a cheaper option than an alternative proposal to build a canal to bypass the bridge.

Teston Bridge [TQ 7088 5326]. The centre three ragstone arches date from the fourteenth century, while the remainder are nineteenth-century rebuilds.

East Farleigh [TQ 7348 5353] medieval bridge was first mentioned in 1324. The southern four arches represent the original bridge, which was substantially rebuilt in the nineteenth century using the original ragstone. The northern arch over the towpath was another nineteenth-century alteration, apparently to raise the approach to the bridge from Barming.

Twyford Bridge, Yalding [TQ 6906 4977], first recorded in 1325. Built in masonry with four pointed arches, it has three massive piers that precluded the removal of any to improve navigation on the Medway. The carriageway is 12 feet wide with pedestrian recesses. The brick parapet is a late addition.

The ragstone Eynsford Bridge and ford crossing the Darent [TQ 5399 6553] could be medieval. A figure, possibly an angel, is located above the cutwater. An eighteenth-century mill stands downstream.

Edenbridge toll bridge over the Eden [TQ 4444 4597] was built in 1836 by the Great Stone Bridge Trust at a point where there had been a crossing since Roman times on the Lewes road. A stone bridge existed at this location from the late medieval period, the Trust with twelve wardens being set up as a charity to maintain it around 1511.

Rochester Bridge [TQ 7410 6890] was built between 1850 and 1856 using cast iron. Designed by William Cubitt, the Rochester Bridge Trust engineer, it replaced a bridge of 1381 that stood 100 yards upstream. The main contractor was Fox Henderson. Originally built supported on arches springing from the piers, which reduced headroom, the bridge was modified in 1912–14 to be suspended from arches above. The short western span was a swing bridge, which was removed as it was never opened.

The swing bridge linking Conduit Street and Brent Hill over the Creek at Faversham [TR 015 616]. Installed in 1878, it was overhauled in 1996, retaining the hydraulic accumulator and hand pump, which lift the bridge to allow it to be swung open using a winch and wire rope.

A stone-built bridge across the Medway at Maidstone [TQ 7577 5555]. Designed by Sir Joseph Bazalgette, and part-funded by the Rochester Bridge Trust, the bridge opened in 1879.

Sandwich toll bridge [TR 3320 5830] was built across the Stour in 1773 with stone arches. It was modified in 1892 with an iron swing section allowing passage on the Stour.

The schedule of charges imposed at the Sandwich toll bridge.

SANDWICH TOLL BRIDGE
TABLE OF TOLLS

		s.	d.	s.	d.
For every Chariot, Landau, Berlin, Chaise, Chair, Calash, or other Vehicle.					
drawn by 6 or more Horses or other beasts.		2.	6.	2	3.
drawn by 4 Horses or other beasts.		2.	0.	1	6.
drawn by 3 Horses or other beasts.				1	1½.
drawn by 2 Horses or other beasts.		1	0.		9.
drawn by 1 Horse or other beast.			9.		6.
For every Waggon, Wain, Dray, Car, or other Carriage,					
drawn by 4 or more Horses or Oxen.		1.	6.	1.	0.
Less than 4 Horses or Oxen.		1.	0.		9 to 3
					6 to 2
					4 to 1
For every Horse or Mule laden or unladen, and not drawing.		2.			1.
Ass laden or unladen and not drawing.		2.			1.
Drove of Oxen, Cows, or Neat Cattle per Score.	1.	8.			10.
and after that rate for any greater or less number.					
Drove of Calves, Hogs, Sheep, or lambs per Score.	4.				2½.
and after that rate for any greater or less number.					
For every Locomotive weighing 2 Tons or under, having 4 wheels.				1.	0.
having 3 wheels.					9.
having 2 wheels.					6.
For every Locomotive exceeding 2 Tons and not exceeding 4 Tons.				1.	3.
" 4 Tons " " 6 Tons.				1.	6.
" 6 Tons " " 10 Tons.				2.	0.
" 10 Tons " " 14 Tons.				2.	6.
For each wheel of any Waggon, Wain, Cart, Carriage, or other Vehicle, drawn or propelled by any Locomotive not exceeding 6 Tons.					2.
exceeding 6 Tons.					3.
Guildhall Sandwich				E.C. BYRNE. TownClerk.

Bow Bridge, Wateringbury [TQ 6907 5275], was opened in 23 July 1915, replacing a wooden bridge constructed by the Upper Medway Navigation Company between 1747 and 1748, which replaced a medieval stone bridge obstructing river passage. The wooden bridge had fallen into decay by the early twentieth century. The bridge is constructed with the then pioneering reinforced concrete, using the Mouchel-Hennebique system developed by two French engineers. Half the cost was met by the Rochester Bridge Trust.

The Great Bridge at Tonbridge [TQ 590 464] carries the High Street across the Medway. It was built and opened in 1888, replacing a bridge with three arches and stone parapets of 1776, which obstructed the river. The bridge was widened to its current width in the 1920s.

Kingsferry Bridge [TQ 9145 6935] carries both road and railway across the Swale. Built in 1960 by John Howard, Dorman Long and Sir William Arrol & Co. to the design of Mott, Hay & Anderson to replace a bascule bridge of 1904, it has a vertical lift to give headroom of 84 feet to allow ships to pass underneath.

Kingsferry Bridge and the new road bridge opened in 2006.

Rochester motorway bridge [TQ 7235 6700], which carries the M2 motorway across the Medway. It was built in pre-stressed concrete by Freeman, Fox & Partners in 1963. A second bridge to carry London-bound traffic was opened in 2003. The HS1 high speed railway bridge to the south, with its novel splayed piers, opened the same year.

Roadside Facilities

Facilities to service the need for accommodation and refreshment of passengers and horses were developed. With bicycles and motor vehicles there was a need for repair facilities and filling stations, met initially by cycle shops and blacksmiths. It was not until the rapid growth in motorcycle and car ownership in the late 1920s that the garage became a common feature. The filling station – a forecourt selling fuel and accessories without repair facilities – grew in numbers with the boom in car ownership in the 1950s, 1960s and 1970s. These were often opened by new entries to the petrol trade such as Total from France and Repsol from Spain. However, the trend from the mid-1970s for supermarket chains to open petrol forecourts selling discounted fuel, as well as the opening of specialist chains offering tyres, exhausts, batteries and repairs, led to the closure of numerous independent filling stations and garages that were unable to compete.

The pump erected in 1769 in Rochester High Street and the horse trough that stood in the High Street, now removed to the Rochester Museum yard [TQ 7422 6874].

The horse trough at Burham [TQ 7278 6220], placed to commemorate Queen Victoria's Diamond Jubilee in 1897.

The granite horse drinking trough on the corner of the High Street and Bank Street, Tonbridge [TQ 5905 4661], thought to have replaced an earlier trough in around 1913.

The Royal Victoria and Bull Hotel in Rochester High Street [TQ 7418 6871] was a late eighteenth-century coaching inn on the busy Dover Road at a time when it was said upwards of seventy coaches passed per day. The central carriage arch allowed coach passengers to alight under cover at the colonnaded area to the rear, and gave access to a yard and stables at the rear of the hotel.

The Rose and Crown, High Street, Tonbridge [TQ 590 466], was a coaching inn on the route to Tunbridge Wells and Hastings, equipped with stables and barns. It is wooden-framed, dating from the sixteenth century with an eighteenth-century brick façade.

The Ship Hotel, Market Street, Faversham [TR 0154 6136], was originally a sixteenth-century tavern, which developed in the eighteenth century into a coaching inn serving the London to Dover road. The central carriage arch gave passengers under-cover access into the hotel, with stable yard to the rear.

The Swan Hotel, High Street, Hythe [TR 1611 3477], was an eighteenth-century coaching inn – the final destination of the London coach. The carriage entrance has been infilled with shops.

When day tripping by motor coach to Margate and Ramsgate was in its heyday in the 1930s, 1940s and 1950s, some public houses specialised in catering for the large numbers of thirsty travellers. One survivor is the Roman Galley (now a private house) on the Margate Road [TR 2258 6773].

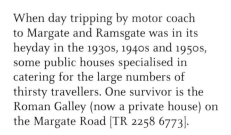

The Old Forge Garage, Penshurst [TQ 5258 4364], was originally a smithy dating from 1891 for the Penshurst estate. It was converted to a garage in the 1960s.

At one time a garage at Mereworth [TQ 6580 5366], the petrol pumps have been recently removed. Now converted to a house, it retains its sign as an agent for Triumph and BSA motorcycles.

Lenham Sports Cars in Harrietsham [TQ 8668 5274] retains its petrol pumps but is no longer a filling station as the A20 bypasses the village. The premises still run for specialist sports car sales and repairs.

The former Lenham Garage in the Market Square [TQ 8988 5217], with mounts for petrol pumps in front of the black doors, was also bypassed by the A20.

Bell Garage was a filling station and repair garage in an isolated position on the Ashford Road [TQ 8187 5491], which is now bypassed by the M20 motorway.

One of two filling stations set up by the Total Oil Company on Corporation Street, Rochester [TQ 7441 6870], which is now closed.

The M2 motorway

The M2 motorway was opened in stages between 1963 and 1965 and widened in 2003. It had a huge impact on travel times on the Dover Road, bypassing the traffic bottlenecks of Rochester, Sittingbourne and Faversham.

Buses

As railways replaced long-distance coaching routes in the later nineteenth century, feeder services in the form of, firstly, horse-drawn and then, in the early twentieth century, motorised buses developed. The bus station and garage became a feature in towns as local services expanded and buses, which were much more flexible in their routing, replaced the street tramways. Often in central locations, their sites have been mostly redeveloped.

Above: The Nelson Road, Gillingham [TQ 7761 6794], bus station and garage of the Maidstone & District Company. Maidstone & District began with services between Maidstone and Chatham around 1908, and went on to become the dominant company in mid and west Kent.

Right: The bus garage of the East Kent Road Car Company, High Street, Herne Bay [TR 175 682], built in 1916.

Railways

Kent saw Britain's first all-steam-hauled railway with the opening of the Canterbury & Whitstable Railway on 3 May 1830. Built by George Stephenson to link the market town of Canterbury with the sea, the railway had to contend with steep gradients requiring the use of stationary engines for cable hauling and the digging of the 828-yard-long Tyler Hill tunnel. Not a profitable line, it was taken over by the South Eastern Railway in 1846 and continued in use until it was closed to passengers in 1931 and to goods traffic in 1952.

An Act was obtained in 1836, allowing the construction of a route from London to Dover by the South Eastern Railway. The line shared track with the London & Brighton Railway from London Bridge to Redhill before heading via Tonbridge and Headcorn to Ashford, reached in late 1842, and Folkestone, reached in June 1843. To carry on to Dover Town Station, reached by February 1844, the engineer, William Cubitt, had to build the Foord viaduct, three tunnels – including the Shakespeare Cliff tunnel – and blast a path along the cliffs. A branch from Paddock Wood to Maidstone opened in 1844, followed by a line from Ashford via Canterbury to Ramsgate and Margate in 1846 and from Minster to Deal in 1847. Meanwhile, the Thames & Medway Canal Company was building a line from Gravesend through the Higham tunnel to Strood, which was absorbed by the South Eastern Railway in 1846. The link to Maidstone via the Medway valley did not open until 1856.

The South Eastern Railway's monopoly was broken when the East Kent Railway obtained an Act in 1853 for the construction of a line from Strood to Faversham and Chilham, which was extended in 1855 to Dover. Construction was completed by 1861. A line westward via Swanley linked the railway to London in 1860. A branch was opened from Sittingbourne to Sheerness in 1860, with a spur to Queenborough Pier ferry terminal in 1876. The Kent Coast Railway, which was absorbed by the London, Chatham & Dover Railway in 1871, constructed a line from Faversham that reached Herne Bay in 1861 and Margate and Ramsgate in 1863. The London, Chatham & Dover Railway built its own connection with Ashford via Maidstone, which was open by 1884.

A number of branch lines were added during the rivalry between the LCDR and SER before they merged to form the South Eastern & Chatham Railway in 1899. In 1881 the Westerham to Dunton Green and the Dungeness branches were opened. The South Eastern instigated the Hundred of Hoo railway, which reached Port Victoria on the Isle of Grain in 1882 from where they hoped a ferry service would run to Holland in competition with Queenborough Pier. They also opened the Elham Valley line in 1889, linking Canterbury with Folkestone, which was followed by the Hawkhurst branch in 1893. The London, Chatham & Dover's last venture was to build a line from Fawkham to Gravesend West. There was one last venture by the Southern Railway, opened in 1932, which was a branch from the Hundred of Hoo Railway to Allhallows in an attempt to develop a seaside resort.

The railways have left a legacy in structures ranging from stations and signal boxes to viaducts and tunnels.

The flywheel from one of the winding engines that hauled trains on steep gradients on the Canterbury & Whitstable Railway, now lying in Gas Street, Canterbury [TR 1452 5745]. *Invicta*, George Stephenson's original locomotive for the railway, is in store at Canterbury at the time of writing.

Maidstone West station [TQ 7557 5538], which was originally the terminus for a single track from Paddock Wood when the branch was opened on 25 September 1844. The track was doubled with a through running track when the line was linked with Strood in June 1856. In the background is a lattice footbridge between platforms dating from around 1897.

East Farleigh station [TQ 734 536] was built in 1844 on the Maidstone to Paddock Wood branch of the SER. It is a rare survivor of the company style, constructed in clapboard.

Canterbury West station [TR 1455 5843] was built in the classical style by the South Eastern Railway in 1846. Adjacent at the north end of the down platform was the Canterbury terminus of the Canterbury & Whitstable Railway.

Gravesend station [TQ 646 740] was the terminus of the North Kent line with a grandiose portico supported by four cast iron columns.

Ironwork supporting the canopy at Gravesend station [TQ 6460 7400], dating from when the line opened in 1849.

Higham station [TQ 7158 7262] on the Gravesend to Strood line at the northern entrance to the Strood tunnel, opened in 1849 by the South Eastern Railway.

Snodland station [TQ 7066 6188] on the Strood to Maidstone line, opened 1856 by the SER.

Grade II listed Wateringbury station [TQ 691 528], built in the mid-nineteenth century on the Maidstone to Paddock Wood line by the South Eastern Railway in Tudor revival style.

Tunbridge Wells West station [TQ 5793 3842], opened in 1866 by the London Brighton & South Coast Railway on the line from East Grinstead via Groombridge, and linking with Brighton and Eastbourne. The line closed in 1985 with part of the adjacent facilities being utilised by the Spa Valley Railway.

West Malling station [TQ 6873 5754], built soon after the line opened in 1874 by the Sevenoaks Maidstone & Tonbridge Railway, which was absorbed into the LCDR in 1879. The left side was the station, and the right cross wing the station master's house.

Lydd station [TR 050 215] was built as an intermediate station on the Appledore to Dungeness line by the Lydd Railway Company and opened in December 1881. The railway became a branch line of the South Eastern Railway in February 1882. The station originally had two platforms, a goods yard, a passing loop and a signal box; all but the station itself and the Up platform were removed after closure in 1967.

Bearsted station [TQ 7988 5611] opened in 1884 for the Maidstone & Ashford Railway, which was absorbed by the London Chatham & Dover Railway in 1891. The design was the railway in-house Gothic style by Arthur Stride. The two-storey station master's house is adjacent, and the goods shed survives nearby.

Lenham station [TQ 8912 5182], built on the Down line of the Maidstone & Ashford Railway and opened on 1 July 1884. The design was based on that of the Bat and Ball station on the Sevenoaks line and had a length of 85 feet, making it the largest on the route.

The 27-foot-long, brick-built shelter on the Up platform at Lenham station, with a canopy to match that of the station opposite.

Lyminge station [TR 165 410] on the Elham Valley Railway. Opened in 1887 and closed in 1947, it is now in use as a public library.

Folkestone Harbour station [TR 2342 3577], which dates from a rebuild in 1893.

Yalding station on the SER Tonbridge to Maidstone line [TQ 6852 5024] is a brick replacement of the 1840s wooden station building, which burnt down in 1893.

Lattice girder pedestrian bridge at Yalding station, probably during from the late 1890s.

Tenterden station [TQ 8820 3353] on Col. Stephens' Kent & East Sussex Railway between Headcorn and Robertsbridge; it opened in 1900 and closed 1954.

Biddenden Road station [TQ 8774 3676] on the Kent & East Sussex Railway, latterly used as an apple store.

Eythorne Station [TR 280 494] on the East Kent Light Railway. Construction was started in 1911 by Col. H. F. Stephens, who envisaged a line connecting with the South Eastern & Chatham Railway at Shepherdswell running to Wingham, which was reached in 1925. The route allowed for connections to colliery projects adjacent to the line at Tilmanstone, Hammill and Wingham, and branches to Guilford and Stonehall collieries, although it was only at Tilmanstone that coal was extracted. A later link connected with the harbour at Richborough. The line was closed by British Rail in 1987, with 2.5 miles from Shepherdswell being taken over by a preservation society. The signal box formerly stood at Selling station on the LCDR main line.

Shepherdswell signal box [TR 2583 4830], built in 1878 to an obsolete Saxby & Farmer design. The lower storey housed the locking gear for the signals and points.

Grain Crossing signal box [TQ 8631 7528], built by the South Eastern Railway on the Hundred of Hoo line to Port Victoria on the Medway. Constructed by Stevens & Co. in 1882 with vertical timber cladding and a slate roof, this is the last survivor of its type.

The top half of Barham signal box, built in 1887 by SER on the Ealham Valley Line, which is now used as a museum by the East Kent Light Railway at Shepherdwell [TR 2579 4817].

Chartham signal box [TR 1064 5521] on the South Eastern Railway's Ashford to Canterbury West line was constructed in 1888 in clapboard with a pyramid slate roof and sash windows to an SER in-house design.

Wateringbury signal box [TQ 6906 5288], built in 1893, is a Saxby & Farmer Type 12 design as used by both SER and LCDR between 1890 and 1894. Other survivors are at Wye (1893) and Rye (1894).

Maidstone West signal box [TQ 7554 5512], built in 1899 by Evans, O'Donnell & Co. A feature of Evans, O'Donnell windows was a single glazing bar in the upper part to provide a better view. The only other survivor of the type is at Ryde, Isle of Wight.

Canterbury East signal box [TR 1472 5725], built in 1911 by the South Eastern & Chatham Railway to a discontinued Type 5 Saxby & Farmer design. This type was usually built in brick, but was built here in timber to reduce weight as it was to stand on a steel framework. The height was necessary to give vision over an overall canopy at the station, since removed. Larger than normal to house a twenty-eight-lever frame, it features square corners to sashes and shaped timber brackets at the eaves.

Gillingham signal box [TQ 7807 6842], built on a brick base with overhanging eaves and shaped brackets by the SE&CR in 1913. In the background is the computerised centre, which controls signals and points on the line to Dover, Ramsgate and Sheerness, replacing signal boxes. Semaphore signal arms are replaced by LED single aperture lights.

Canterbury West signal box [TR 1463 5850] is a standard Southern Railway design in timber to reduce weight that was erected in 1928, housing a seventy-two-lever frame. The height was to see down the line, which at one time had four running tracks, but only two platforms.

The crossing keeper's cottage at Aylesford [TQ 7284 5879], built in ragstone to match the station building.

Rainham signal and crossing keeper's box [TQ 8193 6652], installed in 1959 when the line was converted for electric power.

Goods Sheds

The Grade II listed goods shed at Wateringbury.

The interior of the Grade II listed Canterbury West [TR 1462 5844] goods shed, which is now used as a farmers market.

Tunnels and Viaducts

The hilly terrain in Kent presented obstacles to the railway builders, which were overcome by digging tunnels and constructing viaducts across valleys.

The portal to the 2,369-yard-long Lydden tunnel on the Canterbury East to Dover section of the London Chatham & Dover Railway opened in July 1861 (seen here from Shepherdswell station) [TR 2584 4800]. Other tunnels include Tyler Hill on the Canterbury and Whitstable line [TR 140 6019] and Etchinghill [TR 683 395] on the Elham Valley line.

Horton Kirby viaduct [TQ 5628 6932] opened in July 1858 with the extension of the East Kent Railway from Strood to Bromley. Built in brick, the viaduct is 390 feet long and consists of ten arches.

The viaduct built in 1843 by William Cubitt to cross the Foord valley [TR 2274 3642] between Folkestone Central and Folkestone Junction. Brick-built, it has nineteen arches and a height of 100 feet.

Eynsford viaduct [TQ 5341 6956] was built by the Sevenoaks Railway (operated by the LCDR) on the Swanley to Sevenoaks line, and opened in 1862. It has nine arches of 30-foot span and rises to 75 feet.

The viaduct [TR 2331 3593] that carried the 1-mile-long Folkestone Harbour branch line across the inner harbour to the ferry pier.

Bridges

The railway swing bridge, which allowed vessels to enter the inner harbour at Folkestone.

The lattice girder railway bridge across the Medway between Strood and Rochester [TQ 7407 6893], built for the South Eastern Railway in 1891 when the line was pushed to Chatham Central station at the eastern end of Rochester High Street.

The bridges on the Hundred of Hoo Railway were all standard design for double track, although only a single track was laid. This example runs over Canal Road, Higham [TQ 7055 7388].

The planned resort at Allhallows did not emerge before the line was closed in December 1961. All that remains is the Station Hotel [TQ 8433 7826], now apartments, and the British Pilot public house.

Industrial Railways

Industrial railways and tramways were common in North Kent, mostly linking brick and cement works to quarries and wharves. Although the track has been lifted, it is still possible in some locations to follow the path of the lines, examples including from the Cliffe Quarry to the sites of Isaac Johnson's Portland cement works and the Nine Elms Cement Works at Cliffe Creek, or the footpath from the Holborough cement works site at Snodland to the Medway.

Left: Some of the tramway track between Holborough cement works and its wharf [TQ 710 628], now a public footpath, is still in situ.

Below: A restored chalk wagon, reconstructed from ironwork and bogies found in the Halling Manor Cement Works quarry at Halling. The ironwork was cast by Frederick Cleaver of Nottingham around 1878. Two wagons from the Alpha Cement Works at Cliffe are at the Amberley Chalk Pits Museum.

Aveling & Porter tramway locomotive of 1926 that was named *Blue Circle* on going into preservation. The locomotive, which is now located at the Quainton Road Railway Centre, was new to the Holborough Cement Works in 1926. It is one of the few locomotives from cement railways to survive, most being scrapped upon retirement. A further survivor is *Peldon*, a J. Fowler diesel locomotive formerly of the Alpha Cement Works, Cliffe, now in the collection of industrial locomotives at the Amberley Chalk Pits Museum.

The sole working example of an industrial railway is the Sittingbourne & Kemsley Light Railway. It was constructed in 1867 as a 2-foot 6-inch gauge horse-drawn tramway to transport coal and raw materials from quays at the head of Milton Creek to Lloyds paper mill at Sittingbourne. The line was upgraded to steam in 1905 and the line was extended to Ridham Dock in 1919, from which wood pulp was hauled to the papermills until closure for industrial use in 1968. Since 1970 the line has been operated as a heritage railway. Apart from some of the original locomotives and rolling stock from the line, the SKLR has four carriages from the Chattenden & Upnor Railway, which served the ammunition stores at Chattenden.

A number of military and naval railways were operated in Kent. The naval dockyard at Chatham was equipped with both standard gauge and narrow gauge railway networks. The standard gauge line ran the length of the dockyard, connecting the wharves and basins

Sittingbourne & Kemsley Light Railway locomotives, including Kerr Stuart 926 saddle tank *Leader* (red) new in 1905, Kerr Stuart 4219 saddle tank *Melior* (green) of 1924, with W. G. Bagnall 2472 *Alpha* (in shed) of 1932 and Bagnall 2511 *Triumph* of 1934 awaiting restoration. (Photo courtesy of Sittingbourne & Kemsley Light Railway)

Leader with pulp wagons. (Photograph Sittingbourne & Kemsley Light Railway)

Hunslet *Barton Hall,* built 1965, seen on the Milton viaduct [TQ 9126 6500]. The engine arrived on the SKLR in 2004 from the Welshpool & Llanfair Railway, originally being new to the Royal Navy Armaments Depot, Dean Hill, Wiltshire.

The Milton viaduct, which carried the railway up to the Sittingbourne papermill, was constructed between 1914 and 1915 in reinforced concrete. It is 2,895 feet long in 118 spans with six bridges over roads, making it one of the longest structures of its kind.

with the building slips and smithery. A connection was made with the London, Chatham & Dover main line by a loop to Gillingham in February 1877. The result was a network of 2 miles of standard gauge of track, now greatly truncated.

The narrow gauge network, operated on 1-foot 6-inch track, connected the stores on Anchor Wharf, the ropery, and the building slips. It appears to have ceased operating in 1937. Short sections of the track are still visible.

Ajax is the last remaining steam locomotive that worked in the dockyard [TQ 757 688]. A 0-4-0 saddle tank, it was supplied new by Robert Stephenson & Hawthorns Ltd in 1941.

Rail-mounted Grafton steam cranes on the Chatham Dockyard Railway.

End of the line. The bridge rebuilt for the dualling of the A289 Pier Road, Gillingham [TQ 7757 6938], is all that remains of the Chatham Dockyard branch. It was last used to remove toxic waste from the St Mary's Island housing development site.

Romney, Hythe & Dymchurch Railway

The station at New Romney [TR 0740 2490] of the Romney, Hythe & Dymchurch 15-inch gauge miniature railway. Built between 1926 and 1928 by Capt. Howey, it ran initially from Hythe to New Romney, but was extended to loop around the Dungeness estate. It was intended to cater for holidaymakers, especially from the new holiday camps at Dymchurch. The railway operates eleven steam locomotives, some dating from 1925, and two diesel locos.

A RHDR train approaches the station at Dungeness [TR 0893 1678].

No. 7 *Typhoon* was built in 1927, based on Henry Greenly designs.

Cliff Railways

The Leas Cliff Railway, Folkestone [TR 2240 3550], was opened in 1885 to take visitors the 150 feet to the beach. Initially it consisted of two cars running on parallel tracks linked by a wire rope via a pulley at the top. The system was put into motion by adding water to a tank in the upper car until the weight exceeded that of the lower car. The water was automatically cut off when the cars moved, and released by means of a lever when the car approached the lower station. The service proved sufficiently popular for a second set of tracks and cars to be added in 1890. Both sets worked until 1966 and the railway reopened in 2010 using one set.

The beach station of the Leas Cliff water-balanced funicular railway. The building to the right is the pump house, erected when water from the Folkestone Water Company's public supply, which was discharged onto the beach, became too expensive. Water collected in a tank at the foot of the cliff was recycled to a reservoir tank located to the west of the upper station. The original pump is still in use, but the gas engine has been replaced with an electric motor.

The Grade II listed cliff lift between West Cliff Gardens and the Western Undercliff, Ramsgate [TR 3763 6422], was installed in the mid-1920s in art deco style

Tramways

Street tramways flourished in urban centres in the first third of the twentieth century, but disappeared in face of the more flexible motor bus.

Tram shed at Buckland, Dover [TR 3062 4279], built in 1897. Dover electric tramways operated ten cars on a route between Buckland and Maxton, which expanded in 1905 to River. The system closed in 1936 with services replaced by the East Kent Road Car Company.

Sheerness tramway was established by British Electric Traction, who had built a power station at Halfway in 1900. At only 2.5 miles in length, with routes from the Pier at Bluetown via the Clock Tower to Cheney Rock on the sea front, and to Sheerness East railway station at Halfway, it never generated sufficient income to be profitable. Closure came in 1917. A drab brick tram shed survives at Halfway [TQ 9315 7346].

Trams first came to Gravesend in 1881 with a horse-drawn route from the High Street to the Leather Bottel at Northfleet operated by the Gravesend, Rosherville & Northfleet Tramways Co. The company was sold in 1901 to British Electric Traction, who changed the gauge of the track from 3-foot 6-inch to standard gauge, converted to electric power and by 1903 had extended routes to Swanscombe, Denton along Dover and Pelham Roads and to the end of Windmill Street. BET operated as Gravesend & Northfleet Electric Tramways Ltd. The tramway was inflexible and ran as a single track with passing loops in the middle of the road. It closed in 1929 when more flexible services offered by Maidstone & District buses were available. Some of the 1901 tram depot in Dover Road, Northfleet [TQ 6350 7363], exists in an altered brick workshop area.

All trace of the tramways that operated in the Medway Towns has disappeared. Started in 1902 as the Chatham & District Light Railway Company with a route from Luton to Chatham Dockyard, by 1908 its services encompassed Borstal, Rainham, Frindsbury and Gillingham. However, by 1929 the advantages of motor buses had become apparent. The company changed its name to Chatham & District Traction Co., bought buses, and ran its last tram in 1930.

Services at Maidstone began in 1904, operated by the town council with a route from the High Street to Barming, with extensions to Tovil and Loose completed by 1908. By 1924 the council was experimenting with bus services, and then in 1928 began to use trolleybuses on the Barming route. All trams were replaced with trolleybuses in 1930.

The Isle of Thanet Electric Tramways & Lighting Company built a route from Westbrook via Margate, Cliftonville, St Peters, Broadstairs, and Dumpton to Ramsgate Town station – a distance of around 9 miles. It also built a power station and depot at St Peters [TR 3806 7004]. Opened in 1901, the tramway worked until 1937, when its interests were taken by the East Kent bus company.

The tram shed and stables for the Sandgate & Hythe Tramways Company at Red Lion Square, Hythe [TR 1512 3637]. The service started in 1892 with horse-drawn single-deck cars, and was never electrified. Taken over in 1894 by the South Eastern Railway, it operated until the First World War, after which a summer-only service was run until closure in 1921. The adjacent stables have been demolished.

The side wall of the tram shed, marking the SER takeover.

Carriage by Water

Kent's long coastline provided opportunities for waterborne transport in both coastal and continental trades. This advantage was enhanced by Kent's strategic location, being the shortest Channel crossing to Europe, and by its proximity to London, the country's commercial centre. Additionally, day trips to and holidays at seaside resorts grew in popularity in the nineteenth century with steamboats carrying Londoners to their destinations. These included Gravesend, a favourite in the mid-1840s, Sheerness, Herne Bay, Margate, and Ramsgate where piers for disembarkation, promenades and entertainment facilities catered for their needs.

The terrain in Kent did not lend itself to the development of inland waterways. As a result, developments in this sector were limited to improvements of the Stour to Fordwich, of the Medway to Tonbridge, and of Dartford Creek. The construction of canals was restricted to a small cut across Cliffe marshes, the building of the Royal Military Canal, and the Thames & Medway Canal.

Ports

At Dover, the mouth of the river Dour was used as an anchorage by the Romans who built Pharos on the Eastern and Western Heights to guide vessels. Gradually, silting and the build-up of shingle pushed the river and the port westward, leading the Tudors to dam the Dour to form the Great Pent in 1583, which they hoped would hold sufficient water to scour the tidal anchorage. The Pent was converted into Wellington Dock with lock gates in 1821. The Crosswall, with lock gates originally built in 1689 to enclose the tidal basin, was transformed in 1874 to form the Granville Dock, with a 70-foot entrance between the Wellington Dock and the tidal harbour. Admiralty Pier was constructed between 1848 and 1854 as a breakwater to hold back shingle and provide a harbour of refuge for the Royal Navy. In 1861 the South Eastern Railway, who had been using the Town station since 1851, ran trains onto the pier, while the London, Chatham & Dover Railway ran to the Harbour station. The Prince of Wales Pier was constructed between 1893 and 1902. The landward half was iron trestle and the seaward half masonry. The eastern side was used by transatlantic steamers and the western by cross-Channel steamers. The Admiralty harbour, encompassing 610 acres, was commenced in 1898 and completed in 1909, with the Admiralty Pier being extended to 4,140 feet, as well a new East pier of 2,900 feet and a breakwater of 4,200 feet being constructed.

A now historical photograph taken in 2009 with the Prince of Wales Pier [TR 318 409] centre, adjacent to the now demolished hovercraft terminal, and Admiralty Pier to the right with cruise ships and the former Marine station used as a cruise terminal. The large white building is the Lord Warden Hotel, opened in 1853 by the South Eastern Railway, which is now the Dover Harbour Board offices.

Slip Quay, Wellington Dock [TR 318 409], with nineteenth-century warehouses and crane.

Folkestone harbour [TR 233 359] was created when Thomas Telford built a pier in 1807. This harbour quickly silted and the bankrupt harbour company was bought by the South Eastern Railway in 1842 to develop cross-Channel traffic. The Horn Pier for steam packets was built in 1844 and accessed by the railway in 1847 via the viaduct and swing bridge, effectively creating an inner harbour. The Promenade Pier was built 1861–3 to allow bigger ships to use the port at low water. In 1874 the railway was extended to the 'New Pier', which was strengthened and had a parapet built for shelter from the westerly storms. Lastly, between 1897 and 1905 the 'New Pier' was extended, had double track laid, and an awning over the platform added.

Whitstable harbour was built in 1832 by the Whitstable & Canterbury Railway. Thomas Telford was the consulting engineer, supervising the £10,000 contract with 100 men digging the basin and channel to the sea. Chief items imported were coal and timber. Coke ovens, which were an early feature at the dock site, were demolished in the late nineteenth century. To flush the harbour a reservoir was built just inland, now the public car park opposite.

Margate harbour [TR 352 712] initially catered for the hoy trade carrying grain and malt from Thanet. The carriage of passengers developed with the popularity of Margate as a sea bathing resort from the 1790s, and 1815 saw the first arrival of paddle steamers with trippers. To protect the landing place, a 900-foot-long stone pier was erected between 1810 and 1815 under the supervision of John Rennie. Due to the drying out of the harbour at low tide, a longer iron jetty was constructed to the east for use by steamers, but this collapsed in 1975.

Folkestone harbour extensions, protecting the port from shingle build-up.

The harbour at Whitstable [TR 108 670] was bought by Whitstable Urban District Council from British Rail in 1958. The West Quay seen to the left of the entrance was rebuilt in 1966.

Margate pier.

Ramsgate harbour [TR 384 645] was developed after 1747 as a harbour of refuge consisting of an east and west pier around a tidal basin, which was largely completed by 1850. The construction of a cross wall with lock gates by Smeaton created an inner harbour containing the fishing port and the Town Wharf and an outer harbour. A commercial quay was developed from the outer area from 1973 with extensions to the west in the 1980s to accommodate freighters and car ferries.

Gravesend and Northfleet had been an embarkation point for East Indiamen and emigrant ships to Australia and New Zealand until the late nineteenth century. To cater for the travellers there were numerous inns, giving Gravesend one of the highest ratios of public houses to head of population in the country. Most of the inns associated with shipping and mariners have disappeared with the exception of the Three Daws.

The cross wall and lock, Ramsgate Harbour.

The former car ferry terminal for the Ramsgate to Ostend service.

The Three Daws Inn, Gravesend [TQ 6478 7443].

Piers

West Street pier [TQ 6440 7449] is all that remains of the LCDR branch from Fawkham Junction to Gravesend. The pier was used by the Batavia Line for sailings to Rotterdam until 1939, and post-war by the General Steam Navigation Company for pleasure trips. British Rail withdrew passenger services in 1953 and closed the line to freight in 1968.

The Town Pier, Gravesend [TQ 6480 7450], built 1831–1834 by Gravesend Corporation at a cost of £8,700 as a steamboat pier when Gravesend was of growing importance as a destination for trippers and holidaymakers. Attractions included pleasure gardens (including Rosherville after 1837), bathing (bathing machines had appeared at Clifton Marine Parade by 1796), rowing on the canal, teas at the windmill and many public houses. It was used as a ferry terminal by the London, Tilbury & Southend Railway to connect with Tilbury station from 1854.

The Royal Terrace Pier, Gravesend [TQ 651 745], built in 1842 to cater for day trippers who could proceed via Hamer Street to the windmill and its pleasure gardens. The pier is now used by the Port of London Authority for river pilots.

The interior of the Royal Terrace Pier. The 'Royal' epithet was added after Princess Alexandra arrived here from Denmark on the way to marry the Prince of Wales, later Edward VII.

Piers were built on the Medway at Strood, Rochester, and Chatham to service merchant ships, and to provide picking-up points for pleasure craft.

The original Strood pier in Canal Road [TQ 7415 6922] was built by the South Eastern Railway in 1860, but demolished in 1905. Rebuilt in 1907 by the SER, it served as a pick-up point for passengers for excursions to Southend and Herne Bay using the paddle steamers of the New Medway Steam Packet Company, based on the opposite bank at Acorn Wharf.

Ship Pier, Rochester [TQ 7515 6804], was built by Rochester Corporation in 1883 as a landing place for the crews of vessels – particularly coal brigs – moored in the river. It was maintained by the Medway Conservancy after 1906.

Sun Pier, Chatham [TQ 7550 6805], had belonged to the Best family, brewers, from whom it was purchased by Chatham Local Board of Health in 1864 for £1,500. The present pier was built by the Local Board in 1886 after receiving a £3,500 grant from the Rochester Bridge Trust. It was extended between 1902 and 1904 again with a grant from the Bridge Trust, and repaired in the 1980s. It was a popular pick-up point for steamers such as the *Medway Queen* for trips to Southend.

The *Medway Queen* was the last of the paddle steamers to operate from Sun Pier, Chatham, to Southend.

A wooden pier was built at Herne Bay 1831–2 to enable steamboats to disembark visitors. Becoming unsafe, it was replaced 1871–3 by a pier on iron piles, which was extended from 1896 to 1899 to be 3,787 feet long to accommodate paddle steamers. The pier was closed in 1968 as unsafe and was mostly washed away in 1978–9, leaving the end isolated.

Lighthouses

Dungeness' old lighthouse [TR 0885 1687] was built 1901–4 to replace one dating from 1792. The round building is accommodation that was built around the base of the 1792 light.

Dungeness' new lighthouse [TR 0929 1689], constructed in pre-cast concrete in 1961.

The first North Foreland lighthouse [TR 3986 6962] was built in 1691 – a 40-foot-high, two-storey tower with a coal fire. In 1790, when run by Greenwich Hospital, two storeys were added and oil lamps with reflectors were introduced. Trinity House, who operated the light from 1832, added height in 1890 and converted it to electricity in 1920.

South Foreland lighthouse [TR 3590 4331] was built in 1843 by James Walker on a site in use since 1635. It was the first to use electricity in 1876. It was also the site of Marconi's 1899 experiments with shore to ship and international radio communication. It became redundant in 1988.

Light vessel *LV21* was the last to be built for Trinity House in 1963 by Philip & Sons. It was stationed as the East Goodwin light. Converted to an automatic light ship before being retired in 2008, it now serves as an arts venue.

Deal Time Ball

Deal was the landing place for the sheltered anchorage in the Downs, where inward and outward bound ships stopped to send mail to merchants in London, set down passengers, receive orders and take on provisions. The Time Ball building [TR 3770 5260] was originally constructed in 1821 as a semaphore tower, but in 1855 was converted so that the Time Ball gave mariners the correct Greenwich Mean Time to set their chronometers for navigation. At 1 p.m. an electric pulse from Greenwich Royal Observatory dropped the ball 15 feet.

Deal time ball falling.

Coastal and River Trade

Coastal and river carriage developed to transport Kent's agricultural and manufactured products, largely to the London market. This trade used flat-bottomed sailing barges, drawing about 6 feet of water, which could easily access wharves on the creeks of the Thames, Medway and Swale where the bulk of Kent's industry was concentrated. Cheap water carriage was ideal for the bulky, often low value products such as lime, bricks and cement being manufactured. Water transport was also well-suited to the carriage of gunpowder from Faversham, Oare and Dartford to magazines at Upnor and elsewhere. Return cargoes from London could include ash for brickworks, rags for the paper industry, coke from London gasworks, such as Beckton, for cement works, and manure for agriculture.

The Town Quay, Faversham [TR 0158 6161], with the fifteenth-century Town Warehouse.

Standard Quay, Faversham [TR 019 619], is currently used as moorings by a variety of sailing barges. It originally served a range of eighteenth-century warehouses and granaries. In the background is the nineteenth-century granary on Iron Wharf.

Above: The wharf at Lower Halstow [TQ 8596 6745] was used by the adjacent brickworks to ship bricks to London. Alongside is the Thames barge *Ethel May*.

Left: The crane that once stood on Cory's coal wharf at Rochester [TQ 7475 6870].

A barge dock was dug into the bank of the Medway at Halling [TQ 7080 6288] to load lime from adjacent kilns dating from the 1840s. It was in use by Lees Lime Works until the early twentieth century.

The Medway was navigable by larger vessels as far as Rochester where further passage was hindered by the Rochester Bridge of 1381, which remained an obstacle until the construction of William Cubitt's iron bridge, completed in 1856. Passage to Maidstone was hindered by Aylesford bridge, where in 1824 the middle pier was removed to form a wider arch. The river above Maidstone was not generally passable until the Upper Medway Navigation Company was established in 1740 to improve the shipment of iron and timber from the Weald. The aim was to make the river navigable by barges via Tonbridge and Penshurst to Forest Row in Sussex. The company built fourteen locks from Allington to Tonbridge, some of which were removed in the repairs undertaken 1912–14. It also constructed a tow path, wharves, and sluices.

In 1828 a scheme was initiated by James Christie and the Penshurst Canal Company to extend the navigation for 6 miles to Penshurst. Work started in 1829 on three cuts to the west of Tonbridge, but the scheme collapsed by 1834.

The Upper Medway Navigation Company was replaced by the local authority-controlled Upper Medway Conservancy in 1911, who engaged in improvement works from 1912 to 1914. Barges last operated to Yalding in 1928 and as far as Tovil until the closure of the paper mills.

Below Maidstone, improvement was in the hands of the Lower Medway Company after Acts of Parliament in 1792 and 1802. Allington lock was built to allow access to Maidstone at all states of the tide. A tow path was also built, and after some prompting from the citizens of Maidstone, Aylesford Bridge was improved. In the 1840s, three new cuts were made – the last and longest being between Milhall and New Hythe.

The Lower Medway came under the control of the Medway Conservancy in 1881, which was later replaced by the Medway Ports Authority.

Hampstead Lock [TQ 6868 5033] was built by the Upper Medway Company to link the Medway with a new cut made soon after 1740 to straighten the navigation and to bypass Twyford Bridge.

The 'new cut' seen through Hampstead Bridge.

Late eighteenth-century warehouse at the southern end of the Hampstead Cut [TQ 6899 4988], with a timber upper floor with loading doors to the wharf. This was built after the Upper Medway Company went into business with their own barges carrying coal and other merchant produce. There were wharves at Maidstone, Yalding, East Peckham and Tonbridge.

East Farleigh lock and sluice gates [TQ 7352 5357] on the Upper Medway Navigation.

East Peckham Lock [TQ 6702 4800] was originally constructed in the 1740s. It was enlarged in 1831 and again in 1912–13.

The weir and sluice at East Peckham is a modern replacement for the original weir.

Stoneham lock [TQ 6815 4890] on the Upper Medway Navigation, where the gates were removed during improvement works 1912–14.

Allington Lock, originally built in 1791, was enlarged in 1883 and in 1912–14.

Sluice gates at Allington lock [TQ 7473 5814], built in 1937.

The lock keeper's house at Allington, built in 1883.

The Stour was navigable from Sandwich to Fordwich, some 2 miles short of Canterbury. It was the major route for the carriage of coal, timber, wine and produce from Holland, France and Spain to the city. Schemes to improve the river to Canterbury or to connect the city to the sea by canal all came to nothing, and were finally abandoned after the building of the Canterbury & Whitstable Railway. Barge traffic to Fordwich appears to have continued until around 1875.

Dartford Creek was navigable to Dartford for small craft. To improve the navigation, an Act of 1840 allowed for the appointment of commissioners with powers to dredge, make new cuts, and generally improve Dartford and Crayford Creeks. In return for the work, carried out by 1844, the commission was to levy a toll. A further improvement was undertaken in 1895 when a lock [TQ 5402 7494], 169 feet long by 24 feet wide, was constructed to create a floating basin, but little remains apart from some stone walls.

The Town Quay, Fordwich. The tarred building is the crane house for a pillar crane whose post is situated on the corner.

Canals

The Royal Military Canal was originally conceived as a defensive work during the early years of the Napoleonic War to counter any possible invasion from France across Romney Marsh. Surveying a route was carried out in 1804 and work in digging from Hythe to the Rother appears to have commenced in late September that year. It had been envisaged from the outset that, apart from its military function, the canal could bring income through the carriage of agricultural products and merchandise. To facilitate trade, a lock was constructed at its western end to access the Rother. From 1807 the canal and the military road that ran on the northern side were put under the control of a commission charged with their upkeep, in return for which they were allowed to levy a toll. There being little industry, traffic was light. The last barge to use the canal was in 1909, after which the lock at Iden was replaced with a sluice.

The dry course of the 1-mile canal dug across Cliffe marsh [TQ 720 767] from the Quarry to Cliffe Creek, which was in use by 1795 to take chalk in horse-drawn punts to a whiting works. The canal went out of use when a tramway, now a footpath, was built alongside after 1853 to supply Isaac Johnson's cement works.

The Royal Military Canal at Hythe [TR 1572 3469].

The canal near Appledore.

A scheme for a Thames & Medway Canal from Gravesend to Strood, proposed by Ralph Dodd, obtained parliamentary approval in 1800. It was designed to save the journey of 47 miles around the Isle of Grain to Chatham by digging a cut of 6 miles. The canal company completed the 4-mile cut, 51 feet wide and 7 feet deep, from Gravesend to Higham by the end of 1801, but it was not until 1809 that work was done on building the entrance lock at Gravesend. The biggest hurdle to be overcome was Frindsbury Hill and, after much deliberation as to the route, it was not until 1820 that work began on a tunnel to Strood. The 3,931-yard-long tunnel took until May 1824 to complete. The Frindsbury basin at the Medway end had opened in December 1822. The whole 7-mile-long canal opened on 14 October 1824. However, the canal was not a financial success, largely because the tide rise delayed entry to or exit from the locks at either end, negating any time advantage from the shorter route.

In 1844, the company decided to convert to a railway with the single line track through the tunnel on a platform at the tow path side of the canal. The line was opened to a station in Strood, and leased to the Gravesend & Rochester Railway, which, in December 1845, was bought by the South Eastern Railway. The canal through the tunnel was infilled, and double track opened in 1847. The canal from Gravesend to Higham remained open until 1934. Gravesend basin remains open as a marina, but Strood basin has been infilled for housing.

The northern portal to the former Thames & Medway Canal tunnel at Higham Station [TQ 7156 7261].

The canal at Higham [TQ 7121 7308], where a wooden staging was built into the canal to serve as a wharf for barges carrying manure until the late 1920s. The canal at its eastern end towards Higham is now dry or at best a reed bed.

The Medway entrance to the former Thames & Medway Canal basin [TQ 7427 6943]. The lock and the basin have now been infilled.

The Thames & Medway Canal viewed from the point at which it has been infilled between Denton [TQ 6643 7412] and Gravesend basin. The canal was dug across the marshes without the need for locks, apart from at the entrances.

The canal basin at Gravesend [TQ 656 743], now the home to house boats.

The lock from Gravesend Basin to the canal, now infilled beyond the bridge.

The lock into Gravesend Basin

The lock from the Thames into Gravesend Basin illustrates the major problem with the canal. The tide rise meant that barges were held up at either end of the canal waiting for sufficient water to exit or enter.

Ferries

There were few ferries working in Kent. On the Lower Medway, rowing boats were used between Halling and Wouldham, and between Snodland and Burham. Further ferries crossed the Stour at Grove Ferry and the Swale at Harty Ferry. Another had at one time crossed a branch of the Rother at Stone in Oxney, now the insignificant Reading Street Sewer crossed by a small bridge.

Above: The Ferry Inn, Stone, in Oxney [TR 9421 2882], dating from 1690.

Right: The toll charges board at the inn, which were collected by the inn keeper.

Tilbury ferry pier [TQ 6466 7451], utilising the site previously used by the vehicle ferry to Tilbury.

Airports

Lympne airfield [TR 1150 3542] was a First World War landing ground that became a civilian airport with customs facilities in 1919. Requisitioned in 1936, Lympne remained in service hands until 1946, when civil flying recommenced. Silver City Airways car ferry services commenced in 1948 and continued until 1954 when services moved to Lydd. Skyways, flying to Beauvais for onward coach travel to Paris, used the field until 1974, after which flying declined until closure in 1984. The terminal and hangar areas are now a trading estate, but the lines of the grass runway and taxiways can be traced in the adjacent field.

Penshurst airfield [TQ 5244 4678] was used as a flying field from 1916. From 1920 it was used by civil aircraft, largely for diversion from fog-bound Croydon. The airfield closed in 1936 after an accident with a 'Flying Flea'. The site is now an open field.

Penshurst airfield in 2017.

West Malling airfield [TQ 6770 5530] began life as the flying field for the Maidstone Flying Club. It acquired the name Maidstone Airport in 1932, but was only used for club flying and air displays. It was requisitioned for the RAF and never returned to active civil use. It is now the site of Kingshill estate.

Gravesend Airport [TQ 6710 7150] was established in 1932, and although named 'London East, Gravesend' it never achieved its ambition to become London's new airport. A few KLM and Lufthansa planes landed when diverted from Croydon, and there were some local services to places like Romford or Clacton. The airfield was used by a flying club, by a flying school, and by Essex Aero for maintaining racing aircraft. Requisitioned for use by the RAF, the field was extended east of Thong Lane, but post-war the site was used for the River View housing estate and a leisure centre and sports ground.

Land for Rochester Airport [TQ 7450 6450] was levelled over the winter of 1933–4, with the airfield becoming operational in 1934. Although Rochester Council hoped that this might become a new London airport, no facilities were built. Short Brothers, who built an aircraft assembly factory on the field, ran an air service to Southend during 1934 and 1935 using one of their new 'Scion' aircraft. There was no other air service until Channel Airways flew to the near continent between 1958 and 1964, using the flight control building (later burnt down) erected for an Elementary Flying Training School in 1938 as their terminal. The airfield is now used for club flying.

Rochester Airport in 2016.

Ramsgate Airport [TR 3760 6729] opened in 1935, being used by Hillman Airways for services to Belgium. An RAF satellite for Manston during the war, it reopened in 1952 for civil use, mainly aircraft maintenance, before finally closing in 1968. The site is now the Pyson's Road Industrial Estate.

Lydd Airport [TR 0639 2144] was opened in 1954 to provide a hard runway for Silver City Airways car ferry flights that transferred from Lympne.

Lydd Airport terminal, built in around 1956, was initially intended to cater for the limited number of passengers using the car ferry.

Hangars and concrete apron at Lydd.

The concrete car parks, apron and slipway are the last trace of the Hoverlloyd hovercraft terminal at Pegwell Bay [TR 3507 6400], which operated from 1966 until 1982.

Bibliography

Allendale, John, *Sailorman Between the Wars* (Rochester: John Hallewell).

Austen, Brian, *English Provincial Posts* (Chichester: Phillimore).

Baldock, Eric, *Maidstone Borough Buses 1974–1992* (Stroud: Amberley).

Baldock, Eric, *Maidstone Corporation Transport 1904–1974* (Stroud: Amberley).

Davies, W. J. K., *The Romney, Hythe and Dymchurch Railway* (Newton Abbot: David and Charles).

Dendy Marshall, C. F., *History of the Southern Railway* (London, Ian Allan).

Easdown, Martin, *Piers of Kent* (Stroud, The History Press).

Finch, M. L. and Garrett, S. R., *East Kent Railway, Vols. I and II* (Oakwood).

Garrett, Stephen, *Kent and East Sussex Railway* (Oakwood).

Gladwell, Andrew, *By Steamer to the Kent Coast* (Stroud: Amberley).

Gould, D., *Westerham Valley Railway 1881–1961* (Oakwood).

Hadfield, Charles, *The Canals of South and South East England* (Newton Abbot: David and Charles).

Harley, Robert J., *Dover's Tramways* (Midhurst: Middleton Press).

Harley, Robert J., *Maidstone and Chatham Tramways* (Midhurst: Middleton Press).

Harley, Robert J., *North Kent Tramways* (Midhurst: Middleton Press).

Harley, Robert J., *Thanet's Tramways* (Midhurst: Middleton Press).

Hart, Brian, *The Elham Valley Railway* (Didcot: Wild Swan).

Hart, Brian, *The Hawkhurst Branch* (Didcot: Wild Swan).

Hart, Brian, *The Hundred of Hoo Railway* (Didcot: Wild Swan).

Hart, Brian, *The Hythe and Sandgate Railway* (Didcot: Wild Swan).

Hart, Brian, *The Kent and East Sussex Railway* (Didcot: Wild Swan).

Lane, Anthony, *Front Line Harbour, A History of the Port of Dover* (Stroud: Amberley).

Lane, Anthony, *Kent Ports and Harbours* (Stroud: The History Press).

Lunn, G., *Medway and Swale Shipping Through Time* (Stroud: Amberley).

Lyne, R. M., *Military Railways in Kent* (Rochester: North Kent Books).

Major, Alan, *The Kentish Lights* (Seaford: S.B. Publications).

Maxted, I., *The Canterbury and Whitstable Railway* (Oakwood).

Minter-Taylor, M., *The Davington Light Railway* (Oakwood).

Nock, O. S., *The South Eastern and Chatham Railway* (London: Ian Allan).

Oppitz, Leslie, *Lost Railways of Kent* (Newbury: Countryside Books).

Oppitz, Leslie, *Lost Tramways of Kent* (Newbury: Countryside Books).

Pallant, N., *The Gravesend West Branch* (Oakwood).

Stoyel, B. D. and Kidner, R. W., *Cement Railways of Kent* (Tarrant Hinton: The Oakwood Press).

Searle, Muriel V., *Down the Line to Dover* (London: Bloomsbury Books).

Vine, P., *Kent and East Sussex Waterways* (Midhurst: Middleton).

White, H. P., *Forgotten Railways: South-East England* (Newton Abbot: David and Charles).

Vine, Paul, *The Royal Military Canal* (Stroud: Amberley).

Yates, Nigel, and Gibson, James M. (eds.), *Traffic and Politics: The Construction and Management of Rochester Bridge, AD 43–1993* (Woodbridge: The Boydell Press).

Websites

http:/www.disused-stations.org.uk

http:/www.dovertransportmuseum.org.uk

http:/www.eastkentrailway.co.uk

http:/www.kentrail.org.uk

http:/www.kesr.org.uk – Kent & East Sussex Railway.

http:/www.msocrepository.co.uk – Milestone Society.

http:/www.rhdr.org.uk – Romney Hythe & Dymchurch Railway.

http:/www.sklr.net – Sittingbourne & Kemsley Light Railway.

http:/www.spavalleyrailway.co.uk

http:/www.turnpikes.org.uk